Fashion Design Drawing and Presentation

2

Fashion Design Drawing and Presentation

Patrick John Ireland

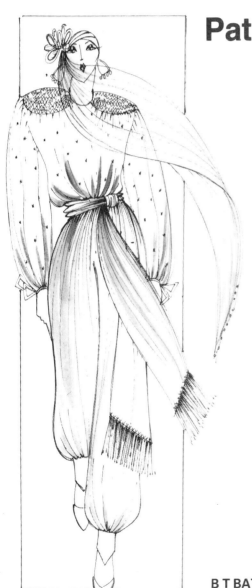

B T BATSFORD LIMITED   LONDON

ACKNOWLEDGMENT

I would like to thank John and Ursula Wilson, Alexander Riessner, Marvita Costa, David Alexandra and Marjorie Dick for their help and advice; also all the students and staff of colleges and residential courses where I have taught, for their encouragement.

ISBN 0 7134 3519 4

Phototypeset by Tek-Art Ltd, Kent

Printed and bound in Great Britain by
Butler & Tanner Ltd, Frome, Somerset
for the publishers
B T Batsford Limited
4 Fitzhardinge Street
London W1H 0AH

Contents

Introduction

The purpose of this book is to help design students and people in industry to develop fashion sketching techniques. I have grouped the different styles of drawing under the following headings:

Design sketching: refer to pages 7-55 and 58-94
Development of a design within the fashion industry: refer to pages 56-7
Presentation drawing : refer to pages 95-113

Fashion illustration: The aim of fashion illustrating is to promote designs which are already complete. The fashion illustrator does not design, but rather illustrates clothes for promotion and he/she works on magazines, newspapers, poster designs etc. Fashion design drawing has many purposes in a student's fashion course and in the work of a professional.

For a student on a design course, drawing is required in the following areas:
1 Developing design sketches and translating them in the sample workrooms.
2 The preparation of work to be displayed for criticism by the tutors.

FASHION DESIGN COMPETITIONS

Competitions are often set for colleges by fashion and textile manufacturers in different subject areas, i.e. fur, leather, fabrics, etc. Usually only the design presentation drawing is required in the first stage.

DESIGN BRIEFS

Often a manufacturer will set a design brief for colleges to design for a specific area of fashion, e.g. sportswear, industrial garments, uniforms, coats, dresses, day and evening wear, etc. Sets of sketches are required at the first stage before selecting the designs which are to be made up.

ASSESSMENTS AND EXAMINATIONS

It is necessary to produce drawings and sketches when taking examinations or preparing a final display for assessment on completion of the course.

The assessor examines the work which is displayed in portfolios and shown on screens for inspection, together with garment samples, toiles, patterns, and research sketch books.

INTERVIEWS

Students leaving colleges and applying for a position in industry are expected to provide a portfolio of their design work, to be shown at interviews.

PROFESSIONAL DESIGNERS

Designers are often required to produce quick design sketches when developing new ideas and when presenting a collection to clients.

FASHION SKETCHING

When attending fashion shows and reporting on new trends, a rapid style of sketching must be developed, enabling the designer to note new trends.

This work involves making a complete record with sketches and sample fabrics of a season's collection by a manufacturer. This is used for reference and frequently sent out to buyers. (Fashion sketchers are often employed on a freelance basis).

It will be noticed that details reappear in various chapters to remind the reader of their importance. A number of specimen drawings are given to help the reader to understand the various techniques and their purposes. Fashion trends and designs in this book have been produced over a period of three years, 1978-1981. The diagrammatic sketches are more classic in style.

Fashion Figure Proportions

The vertical or balance line in fashion poses must be drawn from the pit of the neck to the supporting foot to indicate that the head and neck are above the supporting foot.

It is best to draw this line very lightly when starting your sketch (see pages 18-21).

When sketching you should remember, too, that the average figure is seven-and-a-half hands tall; the fashion figure is usually eight.

The beginner should always draw the nude figure first with very light pencil lines and check the position of the bust, waist, hips and overall proportions. When sketching the garment you will find it helpful to draw lightly a line following the contour centre of the body (see page 21). This will serve as a guide when designing and placing relative details. You will improve your skill by practising drawing from a model or from fashion photographs. As the designer must be able to draw the figure, it would be advantageous to attend life drawing classes and to make a study of anatomy. However, if this is not possible you can learn to sketch the figure and achieve successful results by following the illustrated methods.

The figure guides on the following pages can be used at an early stage for the beginner to work from, by copying or tracing and developing design ideas over the drawings with the aid of semi-transparent paper.

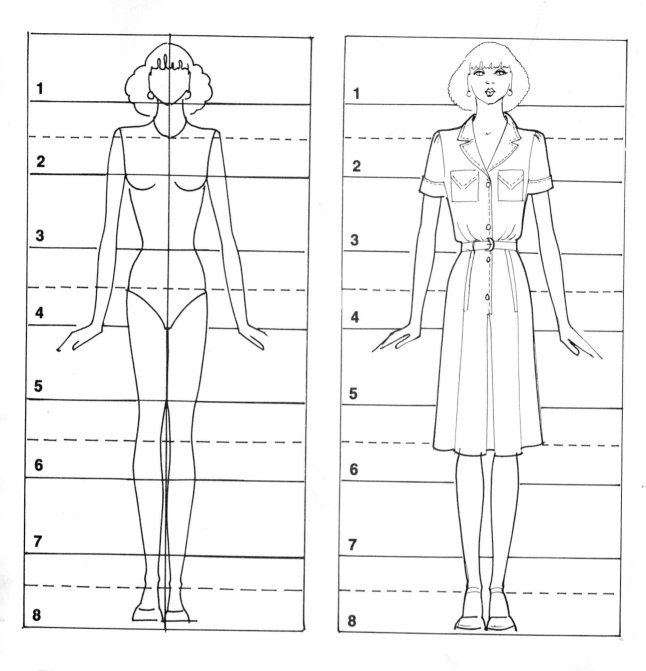

This sketch gives an outline of the average proportions of the female figure. It is helpful to calculate the height of the figure by the number of heads in the body. In the average woman the head will divide into the height about seven-and-a-half times. For fashion drawing the number is increased to eight to eight-and-a-half times. The exaggeration is added onto the length of the legs.

When producing a working drawing the average proportions are used without exaggeration.

At the early stages it is advisable for a beginner to keep the drawing of hands, feet and faces simple in technique.

The four designs have been developed over the figure guide illustrated on the opposite page. Note the way the designs are drawn round the figure. When using a guide it is advisable to consider carefully the shape you are creating round the figure and the way in which the fabric will drape and fall into folds; also the careful positioning of buttons, pockets, collars and seams.

The hands, shoes and heads have been given a simple treatment. Hairstyles have been suggested with a few selected lines to illustrate current fashions.

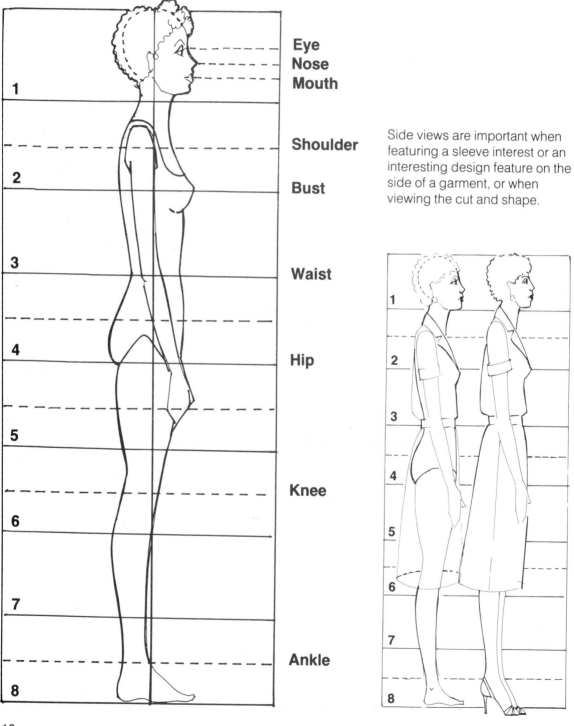

Eye
Nose
Mouth

Shoulder

Bust

Waist

Hip

Knee

Ankle

Side views are important when featuring a sleeve interest or an interesting design feature on the side of a garment, or when viewing the cut and shape.

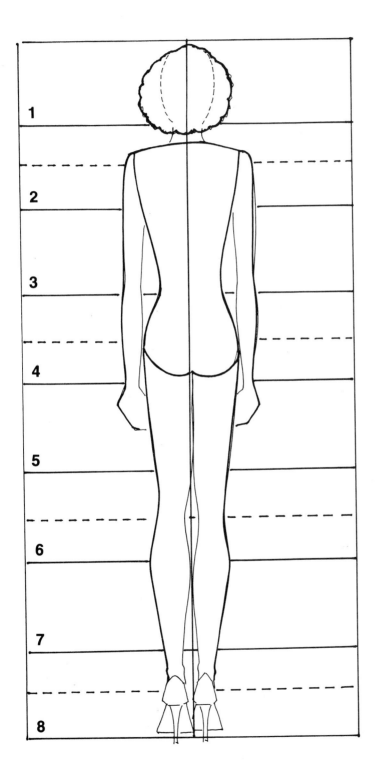

Back views should always be produced when designing. Often students of design neglect the drawing of back views. This is a very simple drawing for the beginner. A selection of back views have been illustrated in different sections of the book (see pages 96-7).

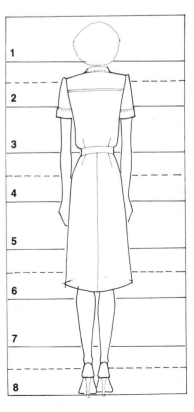

11

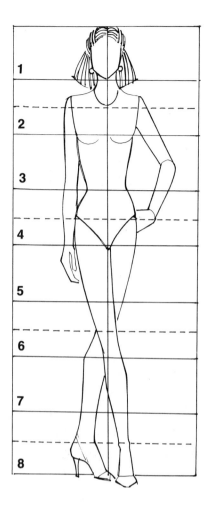

A simple line drawing traced over the figure guide. Note the way the details have been placed on each side of the centre front line. The face, hands and feet have only been suggested.

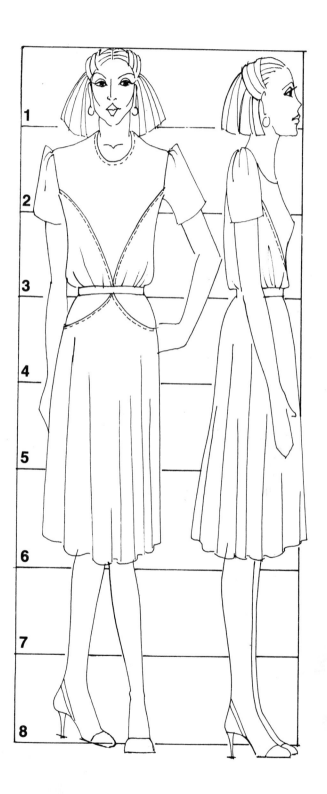

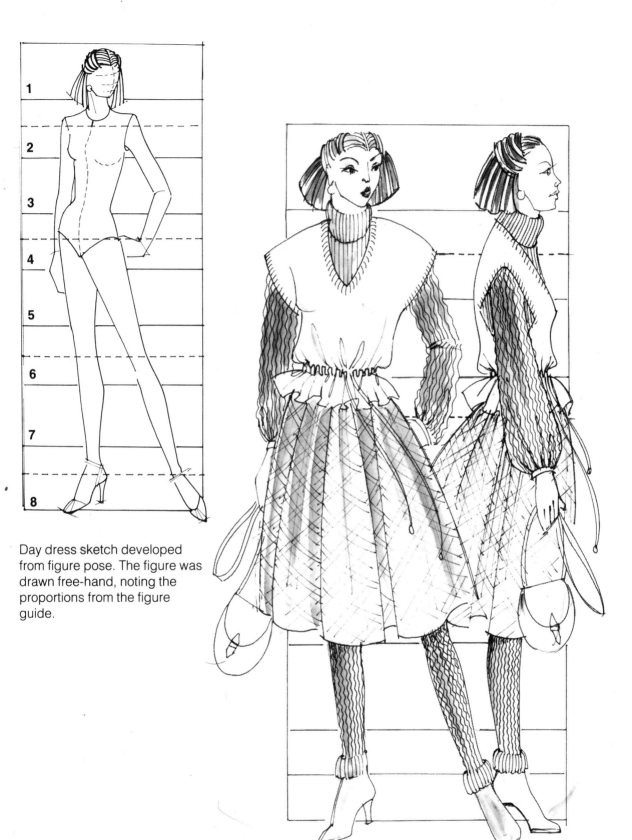

1
2
3
4
5
6
7
8

Day dress sketch developed from figure pose. The figure was drawn free-hand, noting the proportions from the figure guide.

This sketch of a dress and jacket has been developed free-hand from the pose illustrated. The drawing was produced with a fine-tipped felt pen and a watercolour wash indicating the folds.

Note the way the fall of the jacket and folds of the skirt are balanced on each side of the centre front line.

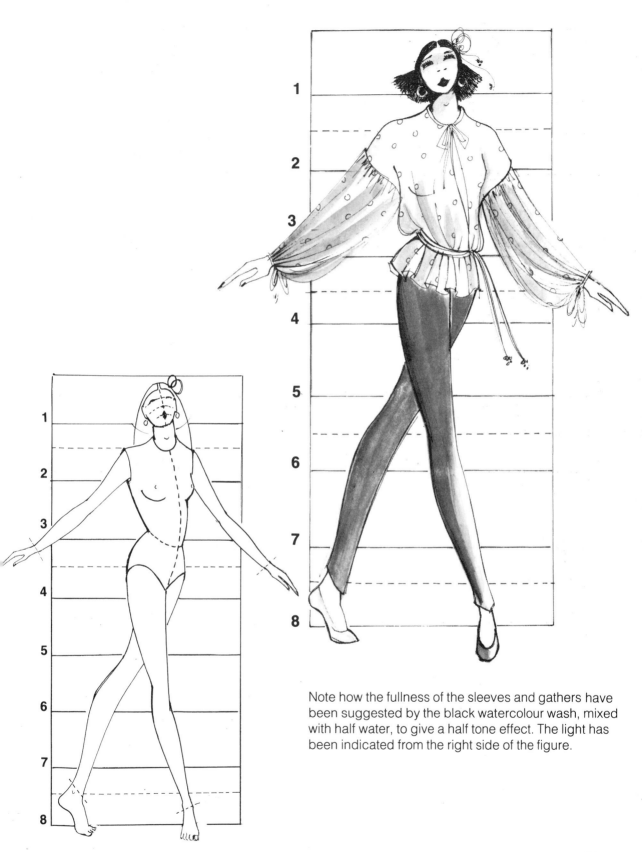

Note how the fullness of the sleeves and gathers have been suggested by the black watercolour wash, mixed with half water, to give a half tone effect. The light has been indicated from the right side of the figure.

Five poses illustrating the figure from different angles. Note the way the balance line falls from the pit of the neck to the leg, taking the weight of the body. The dotted line indicates the contour line of the centre front line of the body.

The details of the jumpsuit have been carefully drawn, relating the details to the proportion of the figure. Note how the face has only been suggested by indicating the lips.

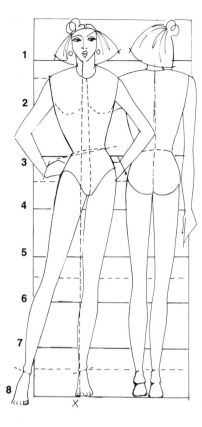

DEVELOPING DESIGNS USING THE FIGURE GUIDE

The figure charts will help considerably when designing. They may be used in several ways when sketching:

1 When designing with the aid of semi-transparent paper, sketching over the impression of the figure, from the book.

2 When sketching free-hand, referring to the figure charts for correct proportions.

3 As a guide to developing new poses of your own, using the method illustrated.

With practice you will develop more confidence in drawing the figure and will no longer require the figure guide. For the beginner this is a successful way of producing satisfactory results in the early stages.

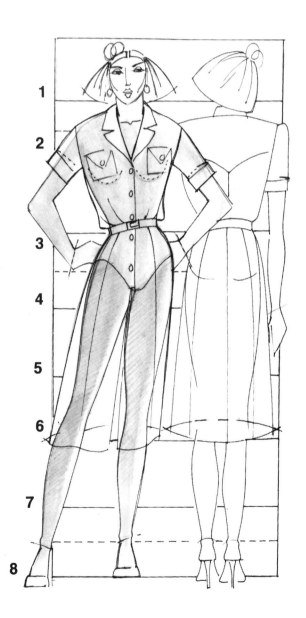

Final stage of a presentation drawing.

Figures sketched free-hand, with a slight exaggeration on the length of the legs. Note the angles of the hips and shoulders and the line of balance from the pit of the neck to the foot, taking the weight of the body.

The same poses as design sketches for draped evening wear. The drawings have been produced with a pen and watercolour wash.

A selection of design sketches illustrating the construction of the pose in two stages.

2 Black felt-tipped pen and soft pencil for shading

1 Soft black pencil, using shading

3 Thick ball-point pen, using a simple line

21

DRAWING ARMS

When positioning the arms consider the effects you require, perhaps to draw a sleeve or to show the shape of an armhole. The length of the arm to the wrist extends to line four, while the hand extends half way between four and five. The elbow is level with the waist on line three.

When drawing the sleeve make sure that it surrounds the arm. Notice how folds appear at the bend of the elbow when the arm is in different positions. It is a good exercise to sketch the arm in various positions, if possible, from a model; or ask a colleague to model for you.

These figures show a slection of poses with various degrees of
torso tilt, depending upon how much of the body weight is being
carried by the supporting leg. A shoulder or hip may be dropped or
raised to express more action in your sketch. The arms are positioned
to display sleeves to advantage.

DRAWING HANDS

Hands are often difficult to draw when design sketching or when working from your imagination, sketching quickly to express and develop ideas. This does not allow you the time to draw in great detail. It is helpful to practise sketching hands from a model or sketching your own from different angles.

From your sketches you can simplify a number of hand positions by re-drawing or tracing over them, using as few lines as possible to gain the effect you require.

A mere suggestion can look more effective than drawing the hands in detail. If you really find it difficult in the early stages to produce an acceptable effect it is wise to keep to a simple line or to position the hand in a pocket or folds of a garment (as illustrated), until you have gained more experience.

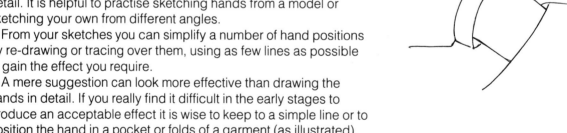

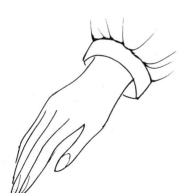

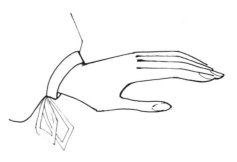

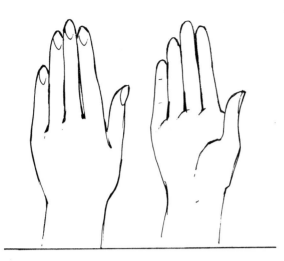

Stylized sketches of the hand

Sketch freely, working out techniques of constructing the hand in different positions.

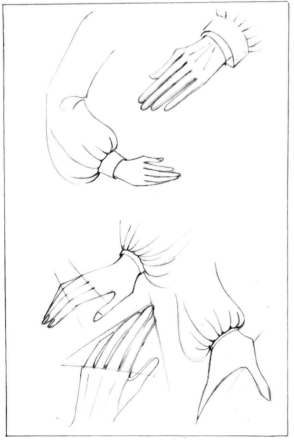

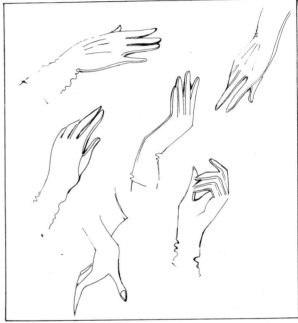

Hands wearing gloves. Note the seams indicated on the fingers.

DRAWING LEGS AND FEET

Only a few lines are required when sketching the leg. Make sure that your sketch suggests the muscles of the leg to achieve the correct effect. When fashion sketching it is important not to over-exaggerate the proportions of the leg in relation to the rest of the figure. Exaggeration in fashion illustration for advertising is permissible, but as you are concerned with fashion design sketching you should avoid extreme proportions as this can affect the balance of your design.

Until you have gained more confidence in figure drawing it is advisable to suggest the legs with a few lines, making sure the weight of the body is taken on one leg when standing or distributed on both as illustrated.

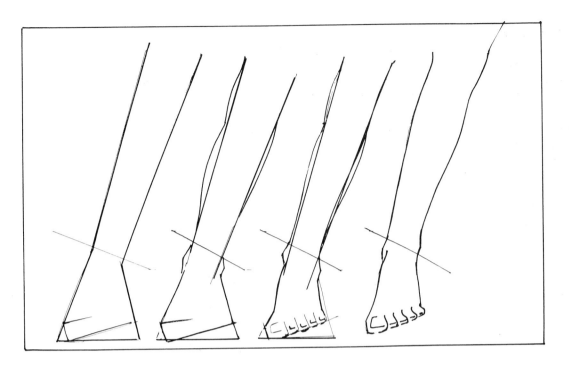

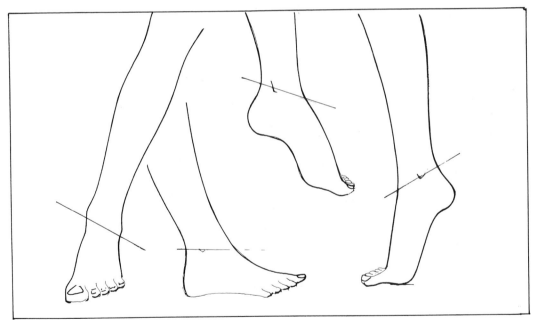

Practise sketching legs and feet either from a model or from photographs in fashion magazines, observing which leg is carrying the weight of the body and the variation of poses which can be achieved.

Using the above method, sketch lightly the shape of the foot as illustrated to indicate its position. This is a typical stance with the front foot thrust forward and the entire weight of the body carried by the back foot. When sketching feet use the centre front line as a guide to obtain correct balance.

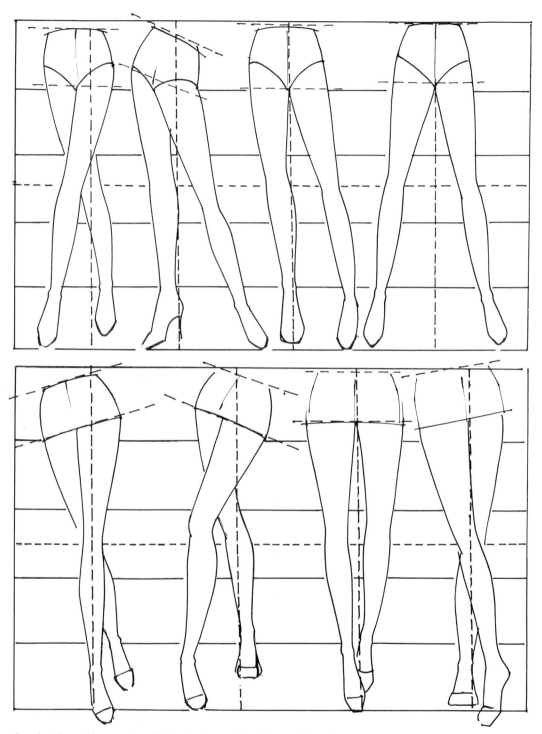

A selection of leg poses. Note the leg taking the weight of the body and the angle of the hips.

These sketches show various degrees of tilt at the hips, depending upon how much of the body weight is being carried by the supporting leg. Hips may be dropped or raised to express more action in your sketch. Note the balance line taking the weight of the body.

The same poses illustrating how skirts and trousers have been designed using charts as a guide. Note the way the fabric falls.
Skirts: 1 Wrap-over 2 Gathers 3 Full deep folds 4 Sunray pleats
Trousers: 1 Shorts 2 Trousers gathered at ankle 3 Tapering
4 Slight flair

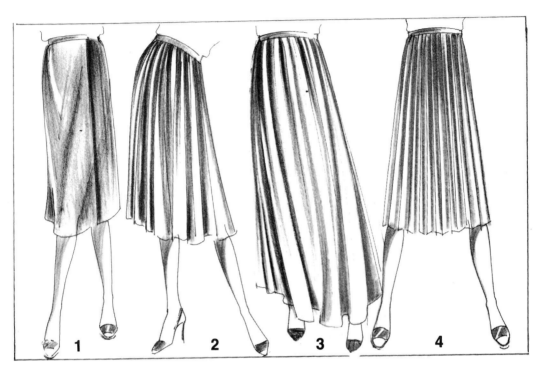

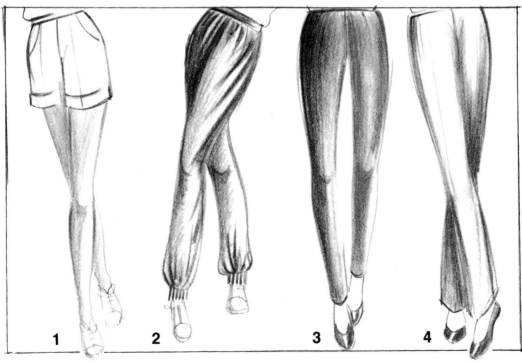

DRAWING SHOES

When sketching shoes draw lightly the shape of the foot first before indicating the shoe itself. As an exercise, sketch shoes from a model when possible, then work from imagination. It is advisable for the beginner when producing fashion sketches to *suggest* the shoe until confidence has been gained in drawing shoes in detail. As fashions are changing you must observe new styles in magazines or window displays. Make sketches of new styles in your sketch book for reference, design styles of your own and observe the details of shapes of toes and heels. Make notes of the current trends in colour and textures of materials and trimmings used.

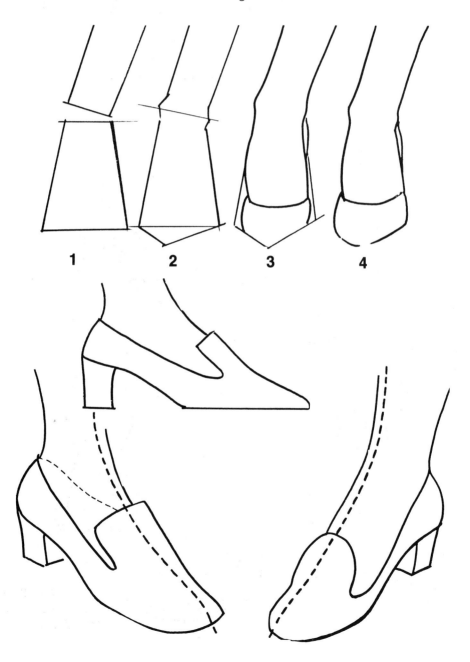

1   2   3   4

Styles from 1979-80.
Town and evening shoes with
high heels

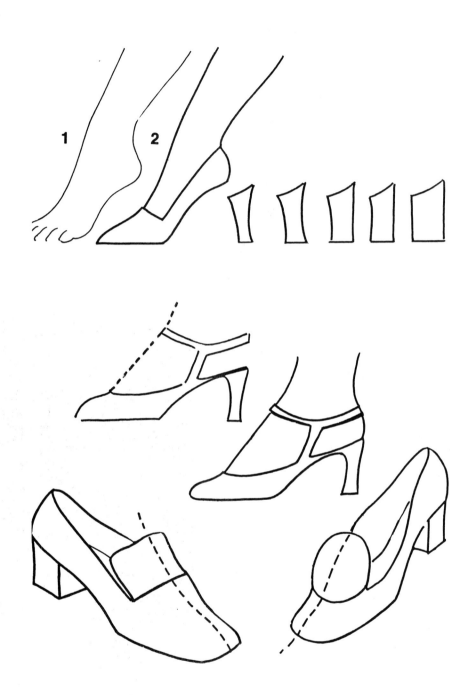

As an exercise sketch shoes from different angles. Always remember to work from the centre front line, as indicated by the dots.

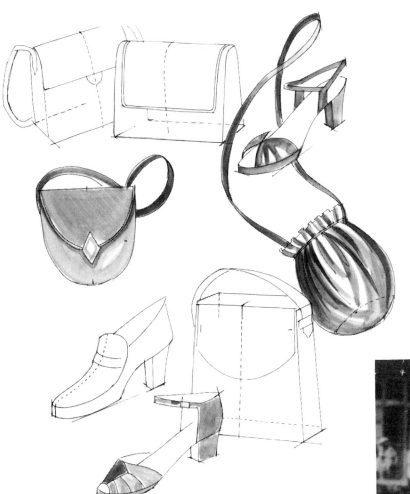

The sketches show bags, sandals and low heeled shoes (1979-80 styles).

Make careful drawings of shoes, bags, and jewellery, etc. Observe the way they are made and the materials used. Accessories are very important to obtain a fashion image.

Photographs illustrating hats as worn in the 1920s, which could be a source of inspiration when designing. As a student of design it is helpful to collect photographs and illustrations of past periods of fashion for reference.

Drawing Faces and Hairstyles

The drawing of the face and hair, whether only suggested or drawn in detail, should reflect the fashion image you wish to project. The hairstyle and the way in which a face is made up should be carefully considered.

The techniques in drawing the head vary from a suggestion with a few lines to a more detailed image.

Fashions in hairstyles vary from a simple, clear line to a more elaborate style, often dressed with hair grips, pins, flowers or head bands.

Observe new styles and techniques in makeup and colouring. Often the emphasis is on eyes, with focus on the eyelids and the shaping of the eyebrows, or the lips and cheekbones. The overall effects often reflect a former period or fashion era, e.g. Hollywood, the 1940s, 1950s or 1960s. Make notes and draw sketches of current looks, collect cuttings from magazines and newspapers, observe and make notes when attending fashion shows.

Use your sketch books and experiment with different techniques in suggesting hair, and the features of the face, e.g. lips, eyes, and nose, etc. You will find as you build up your sketch books that these will become a valuable source of inspiration and helpful reference.

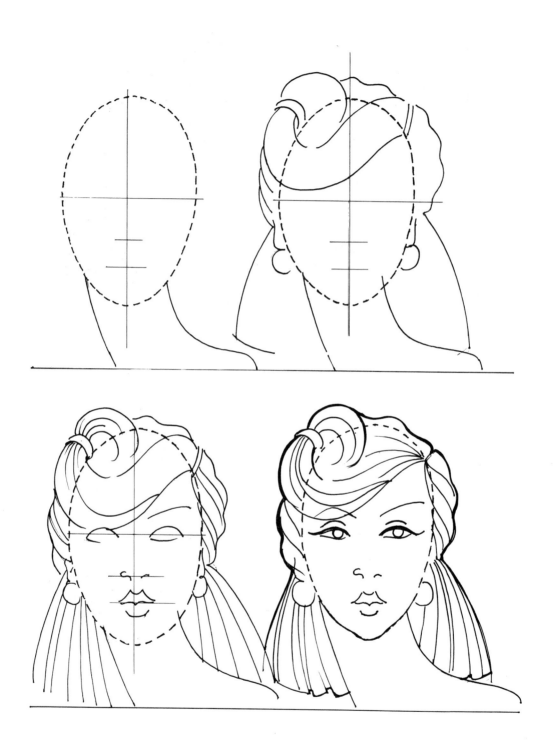

Developing a drawing of the head and hairstyle in four stages. Note the way the hair lines have been drawn in sections, working from the parting of the hair, and showing clearly the way in which the style has been developed.

1   **2**

3   **4**

The same head shown four times, using different media:
1 Thick black felt-tipped pen
2 Fine pen nib with black indian ink and watercolour wash
3 Soft pencil (3B) and light watercolour wash
4 Thick black drawing pencil using different weights of pressure

A selection of heads and
hairstyles using different media:
1 Thick black felt-tipped pen
2 Rotring pen and watercolour
wash
3 Black ball-point pen and
water-colour wash
4 Washable brush-pen watercolour
5 Combination of pen and ink
and black gouache
6 Fine tipped fibre-pointed pen

Heads sketched with a 3B pencil.

Often when design-drawing the features are only suggested, but to do this successfully a study of the features from life, drawing the lips, nose and eyes from different angles, is advisable. Note how the faces are drawn in the section on presentation (pages 95-113).

Drawing Heads and Hats

When designing and developing ideas for hats it is important to work on a design which permits experimenting with different variations. Sketching is a starting point. Designs continue to develop in the workroom when different materials are modelled on a milliner's block, developing shapes from felt hoods, straw, leather, and draped fabrics. Many effects are achieved with trimmings, e.g. braids, flowers, feathers, nets, etc.

It is important for a designer to think in terms of accessories; your designs should create a total look, or a fashion image. Hats may be worn for many occasions: for sports or for day and evening wear.

The sketches are produced with a thick, soft black pencil.

When designing hats, make sure the hat is correctly positioned on the head. Draw with light pencil lines the shape of the head and then sketch your designs over the shape, making sure the hat surrounds the head.

Balance the hat from the centre front line and consider carefully the angle of the hat in relation to the face and hairstyle.

Design the shape of the hat around the head, considering carefully how it will appear from the back. It helps to sketch lightly the lines of the hat from the back as if the head were transparent.

Keep a selection of sketches in your sketch book of current styles and designs of your own. Work with different materials — felt-tipped pens, pencils, crayons and paints, etc. The choice of medium you use to suggest the different textures of fur, felt, straw and fabrics will develop by experimenting.

Often it is effective to combine your materials, using crayons, paints and inks together.

The face may be suggested with a few lines, or developed in more detail, depending on the purpose of the sketch.

Note the heavy black line indicating clearly the balance of the hat and the complete shape related to the shape of the head and position of the features of the face indicated by the dotted line.

Exercise:
Design and sketch a selection of millinery shapes, then take a coloured or thick black pencil and work out the shapes of the hats as they would fit on the head from the back (as illustrated). This exercise will help considerably, when sketching your designs, to achieve the correct effect later.

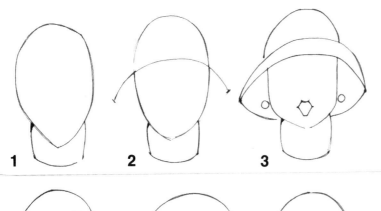

Drawing a hat in three stages working over the basic shape

1   2   3

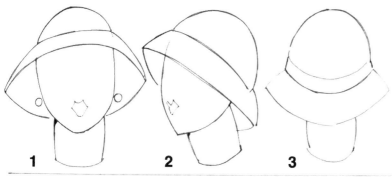

Drawing a hat from three angles

1   2   3

Stylized sketches developed from the basic shape, illustrating different fashion images

You should remember, when designing, that it is important to suggest the shape you wish to express with a few pencil lines. Practise sketching different shapes of hats from a model, working at various angles. If you are not working directly from a live model, use a milliner's dummy.

Arrange the hat in different positions, making observations of the way in which the hat is seen from front, side and back views. This will help a great deal when designing and developing your own imaginative ideas.

44

Note the lines of construction of the head and the features. This style of drawing would be for a presentation when showing a collection. The effects have been achieved using a soft black pencil and watercolour wash with a light touch of white paint on the eyes and lips for highlights.

Felt hat with a roll up brim. Trimming of petersham ribbon

When answering examination questions with drawings, it will often be necessary to view the designs from different angles.

Consider the layout carefully when answering a question, making your answer clear for the examiner to read and relating your sketches to the question when required. Often the sketches need only be diagrammatic, clearly illustrating the written answer. Sample fabrics can be attached to the sheet and descriptive notes added if required.

A selection of shapes developed on a basic shape of the head. This
is a good way of working when starting as a beginner. Keep the
sketch simple, leaving out the features of the face, or indicate them
with a few simple lines as illustrated.

Design Sketching
Womenswear

Elasticated bodice

Rows of elastic thread with self ruffle

Jacket with puff sleeves

Ruffles at waist and hip lines

Full skirt gathered from hip line

On the opposite page is shown a design sheet produced with a fine pointed fibre-tipped pen and colour wash added on a sheet of layout paper. Note how the heads and hands have only been suggested. This is an example of a basic method of working, producing an effective result.

Design sketching and the development of your ideas should be expressed in a free and spontaneous way. For this purpose a style of sketching should be developed which will enable the designer to create ideas and express them on paper.

When working on a collection of garments the designs usually begin with a series of sketches, working on a theme and experimenting with silhouettes, lines, patterns, textures and colours.

At this stage speed and clarity of line are important. In time and with practice the designer acquires a style which is often referred to as a 'designer's handwriting'.

The design sketches can be produced on separate sheets of paper or a selection can be produced on one sheet. Detail notes together with a fabric sample should be added.

The purpose of this work, apart from its use as a means of developing ideas, is that it helps to translate ideas directly and clearly to the design and production team with whom you would be working. There are many styles in which one may express these ideas on paper. If you find it difficult in the first stages to produce the correct figure proportions, it helps to make some figure guides as shown on pages 16-17. With the aid of thin semi-transparent paper which is placed over the figure guide, you will be able to work on top of the lines of the underlying figure.

A selection of poses showing the development of a design.

When sketching, some designers prefer to develop ideas on separate sheets of paper. Layout paper is often used as this is semi-transparent and so enables the designer to sketch over the same pose, creating a variation of ideas based on a theme. At this stage of designing it is important to be able to express your ideas on paper without spending too much time on the drawing. The sketches will vary in style, depending on the techniques used.

When showing a collection of ideas it is helpful to work to a standard size. This will make it easier to look through your work.

The production and working drawing is a selected design taken from the design development sheet.

Note the way the designs have been sketched in a free style, developing an idea working on a theme. A number of sheets would be produced before selecting designs to be made up.

Semi fitted unlined jacket variation of yoke shapes with gathers

Shoulder yokes

Drawstring tie pulled though casing

Gathers from back yoke and waistband

Design development sheet sketched with a fibre-pointed pen and water applied with a brush which causes the ink to run, thus creating a tone wash.

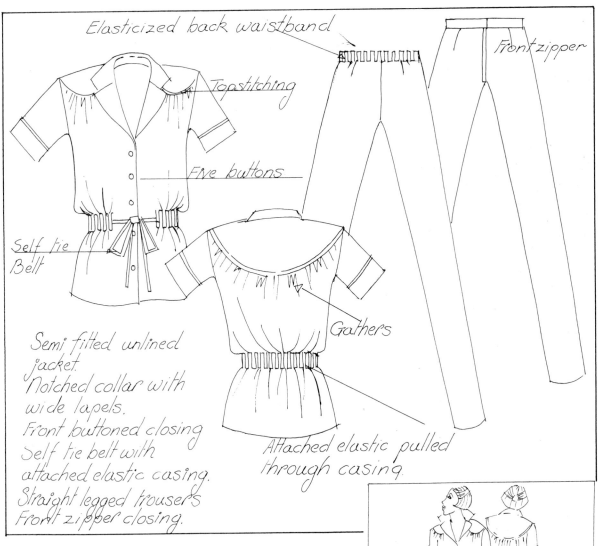

Elasticized back waistband

Topstitching

Front zipper

Five buttons

Self tie Belt

Gathers

Semi fitted unlined jacket.
Notched collar with wide lapels.
Front buttoned closing
Self tie belt with attached elastic casing.
Straight legged trousers
Front zipper closing.

Attached elastic pulled through casing.

Production working drawing

Presentation sketch

Shoulder Yokes
in contrasting
fabric

Narrow collar
and lapels

Full gathers
at the waist

Variation of
contrasting fabrics

Design development sheet — working on a theme

Note the use of fashion design sketches combined with diagrammatic sketches of detail.

This type of sheet is most helpful when students' work is being assessed by an examiner or lecturer, as it enables the examiner to see how the student has taken up a theme and developed the idea, considering cut and detail, fabrics selected for suitability, texture and colours. In some instances detailed sketches of the source of inspiration i.e. costume detail from past fashion periods, decoration, etc. would be included together with samples of embroidery, knitting and trimmings.

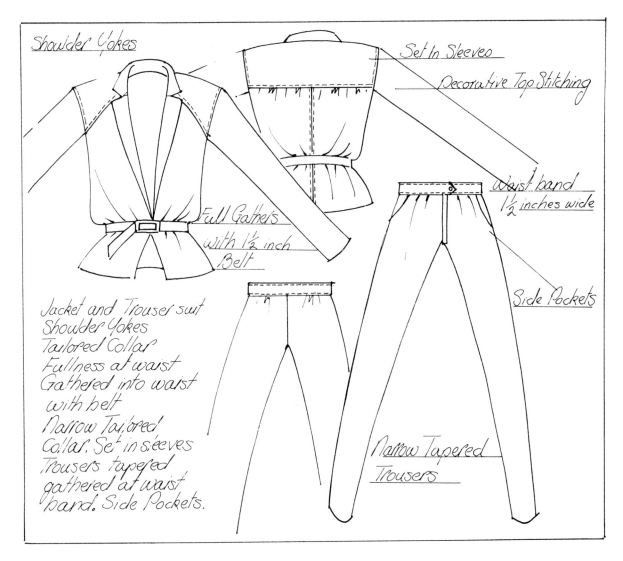

Shoulder Yokes

Set In Sleeves

Decorative Top Stitching

Full Gathers with 1½ inch Belt

Waist band 1½ inches wide

Side Pockets

Jacket and Trouser suit
Shoulder Yokes
Tailored Collar
Fullness at waist
Gathered into waist
with belt
Narrow Tailored
Collar. Set in sleeves
Trousers tapered
gathered at waist
band. Side Pockets.

Narrow Tapered Trousers

Production drawing of a design selected from the development sheet

Design sheet produced in a sketch book. Consideration has been given to the arrangement of the figures and details, and notes on fabrics have been given. Fine tipped Pentel pen with watercolour wash has been used, working on smooth-surface drawing paper.

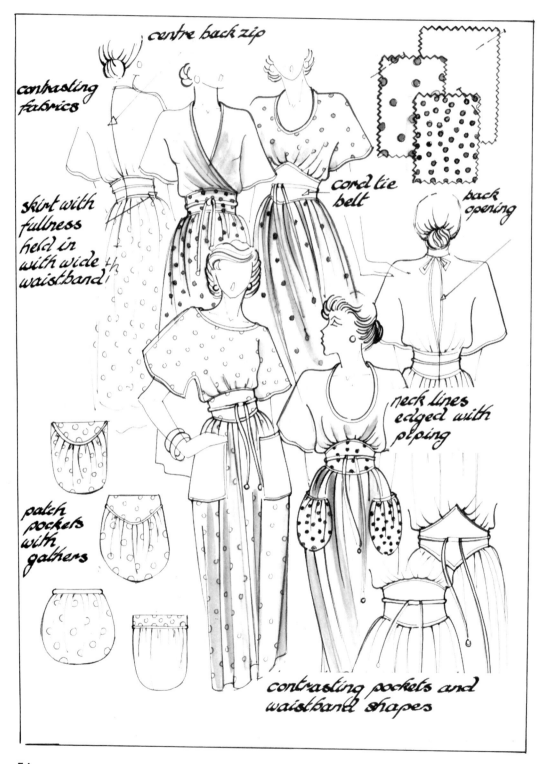

centre back zip

contrasting fabrics

cord tie belt

back opening

skirt with fullness held in with wide waistband

neck lines edged with piping

patch pockets with gathers

contrasting pockets and waistband shapes

Another way of working is to use single sheets of paper with one design only on each sheet, showing front and back views and attaching fabric samples. When showing a collection of design ideas, keep the sketches the same size.

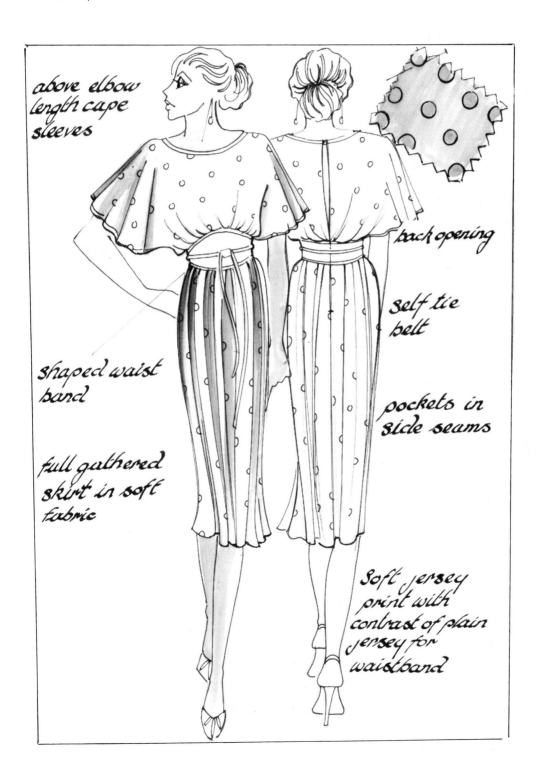

above elbow length cape sleeves

shaped waist band

full gathered skirt in soft fabric

back opening

self tie belt

pockets in side seams

Soft jersey print with contrast of plain jersey for waistband

Development of a Design within the Fashion Industry

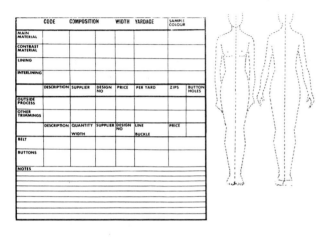

	CODE	COMPOSITION	WIDTH	YARDAGE	SAMPLE COLOUR	
MAIN MATERIAL						
CONTRAST MATERIAL						
LINING						
INTERLINING						

	DESCRIPTION	SUPPLIER	DESIGN NO	PRICE	PER YARD	ZIPS	BUTTON HOLES
OUTSIDE PROCESS							
OTHER TRIMMINGS							

	DESCRIPTION	QUANTITY WIDTH	SUPPLIER	DESIGN NO	LINE BUCKLE	PRICE
BELT						
BUTTONS						

NOTES

This is an example of a production sheet as used in industry. It gives details of the garment costing, i.e. materials, trimmings, yardage, sample colour, lining, interlining, etc. Notice the two figures shown on the chart. These will be used for illustrating the garment and for making sure that every detail is accurate (i.e. placing of darts, seams, pockets, buttons, etc.).

Fashion designers work in different conditions depending on the size of the company and the fashion market for which they are catering. The number of staff employed and the stages of a design may vary according to the size and organization of the company.

The designer should have an understanding of all the different aspects of creative designing and of the sources of inspiration, and a complete knowledge of the different areas of fashion, e.g. children's wear, sports, day and evening wear, etc. Some designers tend to specialize in a particular area of fashion, while others are able to adapt designs in a number of different areas.

It is important to understand how a design is developed for production from the early stages of creating ideas, working in different areas of research such as the history of costume colour, influences of other countries and environments etc., design sketching, developing ideas, and selecting fabrics, trimmings and colours for future fashion trends. A knowledge of how to use the many techniques of embroidery and applied decoration is important. Creating a fashion image requires the designing or selecting of fashion accessories to complement the design. A sound knowledge of pattern cutting and methods of making up is essential, from cutting the first pattern, making toiles and modelling on the dress stand and producing sample garments to the stages of assembly for mass production. Also included must be a knowledge of grading patterns to different sizes, costing garments and marketing. The work mentioned is often very specialized and the designer would not necessarily be expected to produce sample garments or cut production patterns. But he would be required to understand all the different aspects of producing a garment from the early stages to the final production.

The number of design staff employed in a studio would vary depending on the size and organization of the company. The following section shows how a design would evolve from the early stages to the completed garment leaving the factory.

THE DESIGN STUDIO

In a large studio the staff would consist of a number of chief designers working under the firm's general supervision. Each designer usually specializes in a selected area such as outerwear, day dresses, eveningwear, sportswear, etc. Working with them will be a team of senior designers, qualified designers and several trainees.

The designers make their own paper patterns for the first sample from the original selected sketches and these are then cut out by design-room assistants. Sample machinists are trained to report back any parts which fail to assemble well.

The samples at this stage are intended for style and costing. A record is kept of styles produced in the form of a clear, fluid sketch, often diagrammatic with swatches of fabric and trimmings attached and any other relevant details.

Sometimes sketchers are employed on a freelance basis to make sketches of a complete season's collection for reference and to show customers. Sample garments are often shown as well. These sketches must be clearly drawn otherwise they can be very misleading.

The designer may work from the fabric initially or produce the designs and select the suitable fabrics afterwards. Fabrics are usually selected in good time for delivery dates, so as to coincide with the smooth flow in production. Colours, patterns and textures are carefully considered. Generally a fabric length is sampled and tested before any large quantities are ordered.

Trimmings are carefully selected and many effects can be achieved on machines, e.g. quilting, smocking, shirring and different types of decorative stitching, and fused motives. All belts, buckles, clasps, zips, braids, buttons and ribbons are selected with great attention to detail as an intrinsic part of the design. The design team meets to discuss new fabrics and future trends. Designers often attend international fashion and textile exhibitions.

When garments have been chosen from the samples to be produced in the factory, they are re-made for exact assembly methods and fit, possibly with alterations. The pattern, usually size 12, is drafted by one of the pattern cutters.

Once the factory sample has been approved for cut, fit and standard of making, the patterns are graded into sizes. The next stage will be to work out the plan to decide the most economical way of cutting the pattern pieces from the material. Large firms generally have a computerized system for grading, lay planning and marker making.

Costings are carried out in the design department and are estimated on a standard time value for each operation based on the methods sheet. This is then linked with the estimate of trimming and fabric. Then follows the discussion on sales and marketing; this also embraces display and advertising.

Before the selling season fashion shows for buyers are staged to promote the new ranges for the season. The shows usually take place in wholesale showrooms, hotels, and exhibition halls. These shows are usually organized through agencies and the garments modelled by professionals.

There is a wide range of retail outlets for clothes, from the small exclusive boutique selling the orginal design to departmental stores, chain and mail order houses. Some manufacturers retail through their own shops while others employ wholesale houses.

Design Sketching Menswear

Keep a sketch book of figure drawings. Practise working in different media: pen and ink, pencil, crayon, felt-tipped pens, etc. Whenever possible, sketch from life or photographs. Once you have achieved a number of suitable figure poses on which to design, you will find it possible to adapt

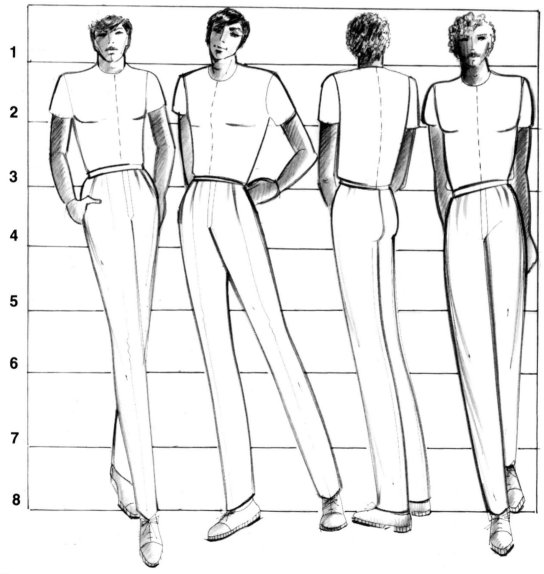

the figure into other positions.

Experiment with the construction of the figures, developing different poses and giving them more movement. Note how the poses have been constructed. The lines indicate the basic construction. The balance line falls from the pit of the neck to the foot taking the weight of the pose; the centre front line follows the contour of the figure. These developed poses illustrate a leisure outfit. The head, face, arms and shoes are only indicated.

With practice you will gain confidence and develop a style of drawing of your own, but at first it is important to experiment as much as possible. Some students may have more ability in drawing than others, but in time and with practice an assured technique can be achieved. The figures illustrated have been sketched with a free line, but figure proportions and basic construction have been observed.

A variation of poses based on eight heads to the figure

A design sheet developing ideas based on a casual sports shirt in
striped cotton and plain fabrics introducing yokes, pockets, and
gathers. The effect has been produced with a Rotring pen.

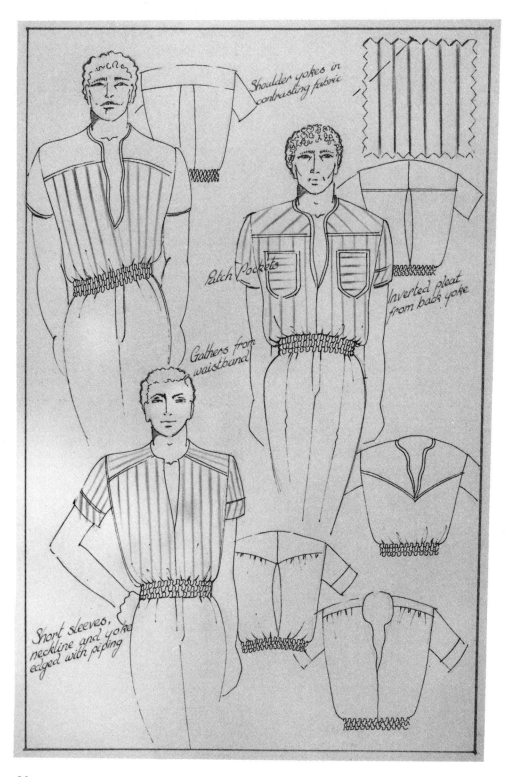

Shoulder yokes in contrasting fabric

Patch Pockets

Inverted pleat from back yoke

Gathers from waistband

Short sleeves, neckline and yoke edged with piping

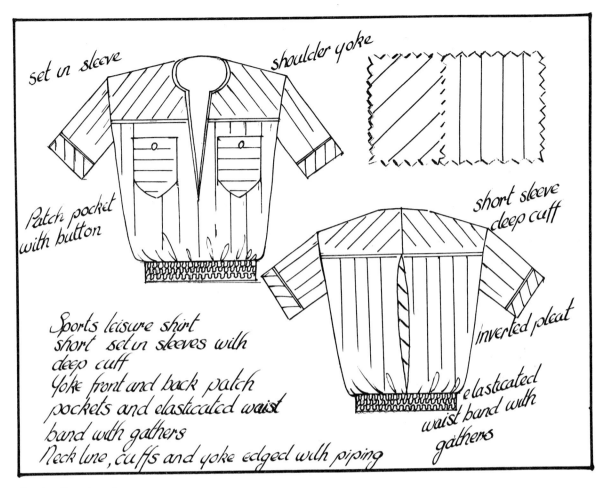

set in sleeve

shoulder yoke

short sleeve deep cuff

Patch pocket with button

inverted pleat

Sports leisure shirt
short set in sleeves with
deep cuff
Yoke front and back patch
pockets and elasticated waist
band with gathers
Neck line, cuffs and yoke edged with piping

elasticated waist band with gathers

Production drawing

Presentation drawing

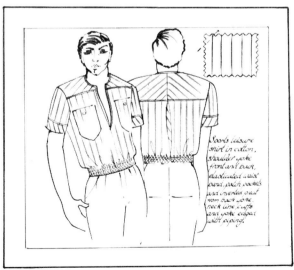

Sports leisure
shirt in cotton,
shoulder yoke
front and back,
elasticated waist
band, patch pockets
and inverted pleat
from back yoke.
neck line, cuffs
and yoke edged
with piping.

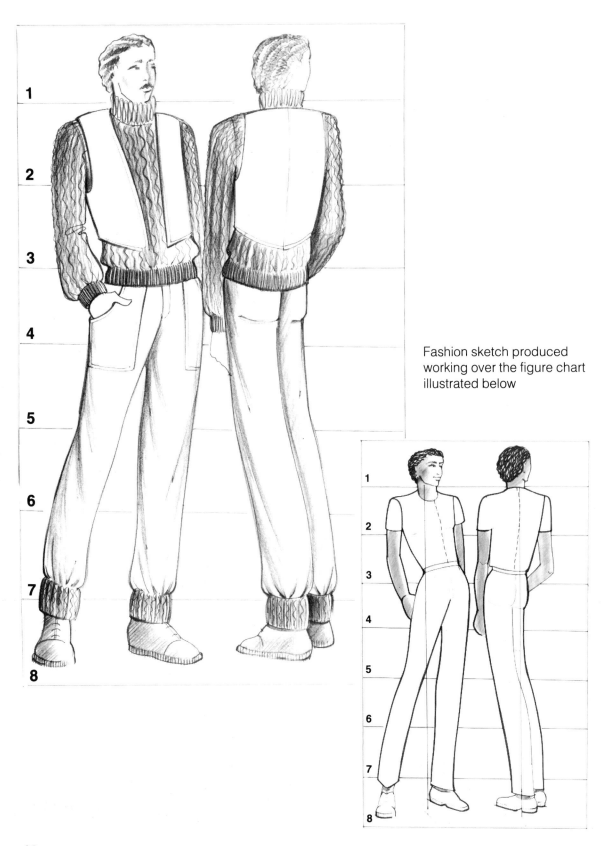

1

2

3

4

5

6

7

8

Fashion sketch produced
working over the figure chart
illustrated below

1

2

3

4

5

6

7

8

Design Sketching Children's Wear

When drawing and designing children's fashions one of the first considerations is the proportions of the growing child. The method illustrated will help the student to sketch the figure and work out the correct proportions related to age. For the beginner it is helpful to work from the charts on pages 65-6, using the method of calculating the number of heads that would fit into the length of the body. Note the size of the head and the length of arms, legs and feet according to the age.

It is helpful to work from the book to make drawings of each age group, then to practise by sketching the figures from memory. Make figure charts over which you can design with the aid of a semi-transparent paper. This will help in the early stages of designing to express your ideas on paper.

If possible draw from life. Note the way in which children walk, move, run and jump. It is difficult to draw children in set poses. It is better to make sketches from life and then develop them.

When design sketching it is effective to stylize your drawings, projecting a fashion design sketch, from a realistic to a more stylized drawing. When design sketching it is important not to exaggerate the proportions of the figure. Experiment with different paints, crayons, pencils, felt-tipped pens and magic markers, using different papers. Work out methods of achieving textures and patterns, suggesting the effects of knitting, woven fabrics, fur, etc.

Design sketches developed
from photographs, taking a
detail from a past period of
fashion.

Figure proportions 1-10 years

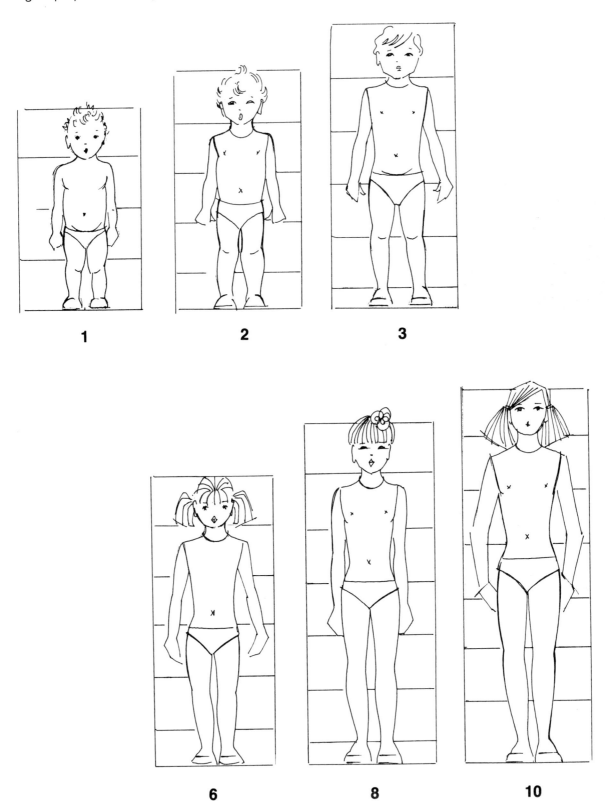

1 **2** **3**

6 **8** **10**

Figure proportions 12-15 years

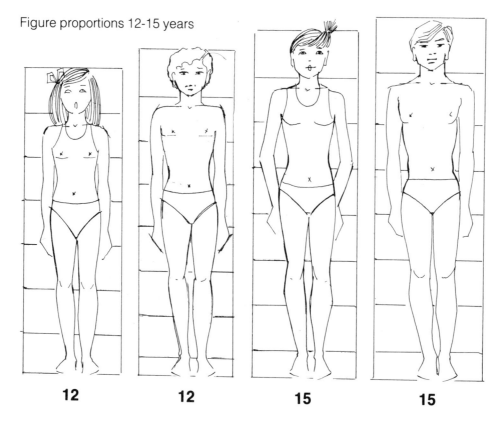

12   **12**   **15**   **15**

Four designs working over the figure guide with transparent paper

Note the stylized techniques adopted in the fashion sketch, using the same pose to develop an idea based on a theme. The proportions have been observed from the figure chart for age group eight years.

A design development sheet—Rotring pen and watercolour
wash. A collection of summer outfits made in two fabrics of plain
and a patchwork-patterned cotton lawn. Note the way the ideas are
developed, working on an idea using the contrasting fabrics, yoke
interest and gathers. When starting on a collection of design
sketches the designer would work in a sketch book or on sheets of
separate paper. Notes, details, back views and fabric samples
would be added. The sheets would be used when selecting ideas
to be taken on to a further stage. It is effective to keep the same
design theme on a sheet using a colour scheme and the same
technique of drawing.

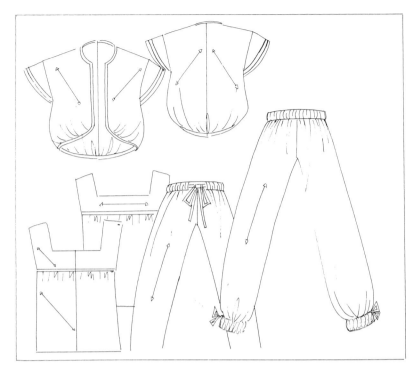

Working drawing of a playsuit, using clear lines and arrows to indicate the cut of the fabric.

Presentation drawing of the summer cotton playusuit in a plain and patchwork-patterned fabric. When a design has a number of coordinated garments, it is important to show all parts of the outfit, back and front, as illustrated.

Note the way in which the figures have been arranged within the frame. This type of presentation is suitable for display, assessment and competitions.

Play suit worn with short sleeve jacket. Sleeveless top with yoke and gathers, drawn in at waist and ankle.
Jacket in a patch work print with set in sleeves of contrasting fabric.

Detail sketches for reference. Experiment in your sketch book with ideas and the drawing of details. Develop ways of sketching the effects of smocking, quilting etc. Design details of collars, pockets and sleeves. Work with different materials to achieve the many effects of patterns and textures. Collect sample fabrics and trimmings and any references which would later be used as a source of inspiration, e.g. old photographs, post cards and costume sketches.

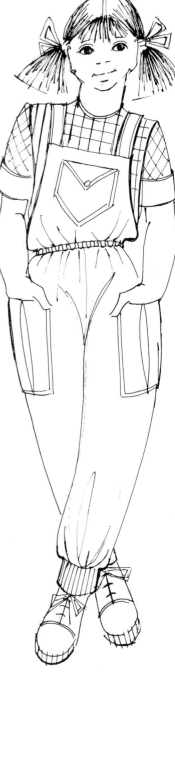

Basic Drawing of Fashion Details

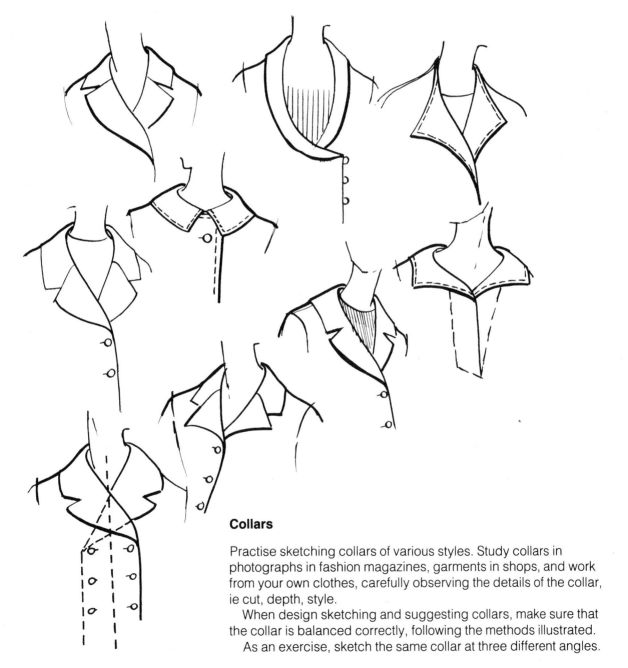

Collars

Practise sketching collars of various styles. Study collars in photographs in fashion magazines, garments in shops, and work from your own clothes, carefully observing the details of the collar, ie cut, depth, style.

When design sketching and suggesting collars, make sure that the collar is balanced correctly, following the methods illustrated.

As an exercise, sketch the same collar at three different angles.

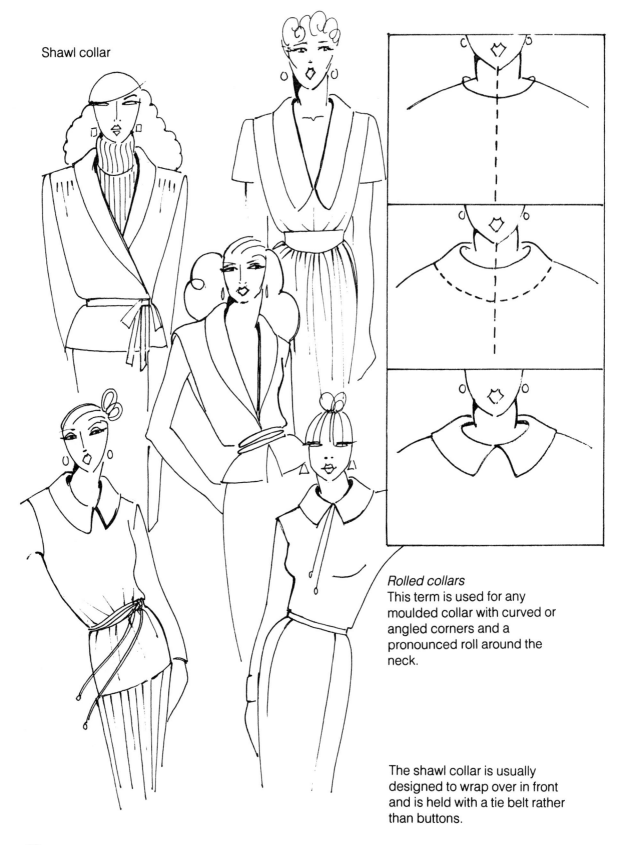

Shawl collar

Rolled collars
This term is used for any moulded collar with curved or angled corners and a pronounced roll around the neck.

The shawl collar is usually designed to wrap over in front and is held with a tie belt rather than buttons.

Double-breasted tailored collar

Tailored collars
Double- and single-breasted collars are obtained by careful seaming, cutting and pressing in the tradition of the tailor's craft.

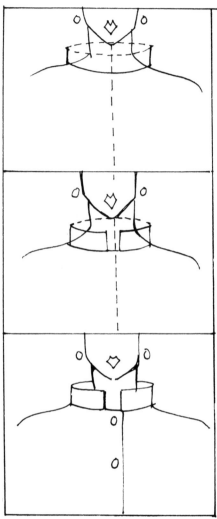

Stand collar
Stand collar meeting at the front of the neck as seen in mandarin dress. Many variations may be designed from this style.

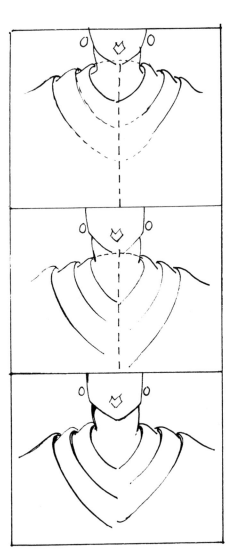

Cowl necklines
A soft, draped neckline. The bodice front or back is cut on the bias of the fabric to drape in soft folds, or a piece may be arranged to drape on top of the bodice.

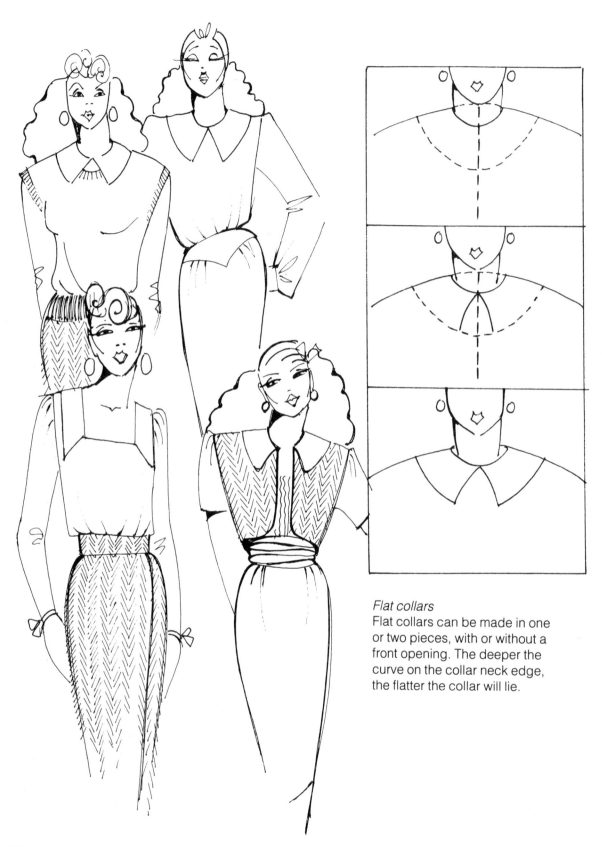

Flat collars
Flat collars can be made in one
or two pieces, with or without a
front opening. The deeper the
curve on the collar neck edge,
the flatter the collar will lie.

SLEEVES

When drawing the sleeve, make sure that it surrounds the arm.
Notice how folds appear at the elbow when the arm is bent in
different positions. Practise sketching a variety of sleeves, varying
your design and suggesting different materials to convey the feel
and behaviour of the material in your sketch. It is a good exercise to
sketch different sleeves, if possible, from a model: ask a colleague
to model for you. Observe the cut and the characteristics of a
number of sleeves and express this idea by using as few lines as
possible.

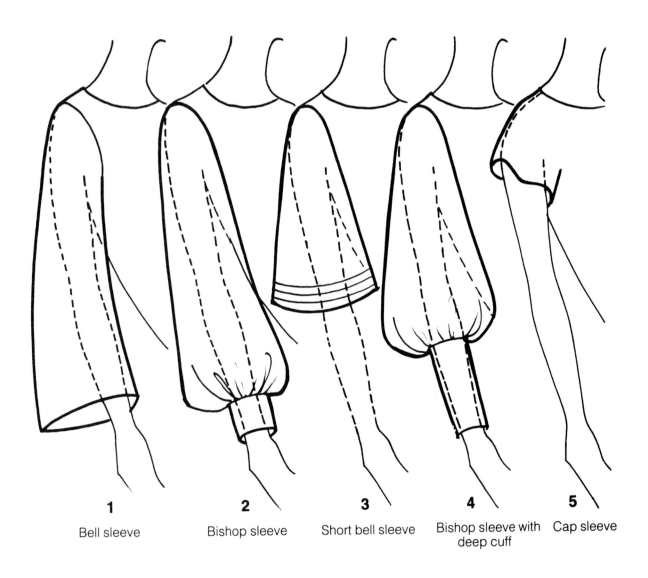

1
Bell sleeve

2
Bishop sleeve

3
Short bell sleeve

4
Bishop sleeve with
deep cuff

5
Cap sleeve

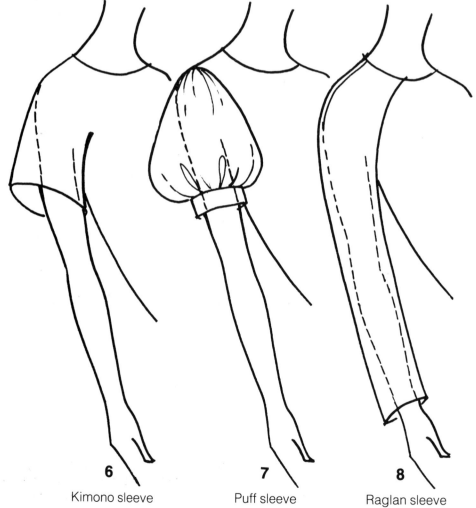

6

Kimono sleeve

7

Puff sleeve

8

Raglan sleeve

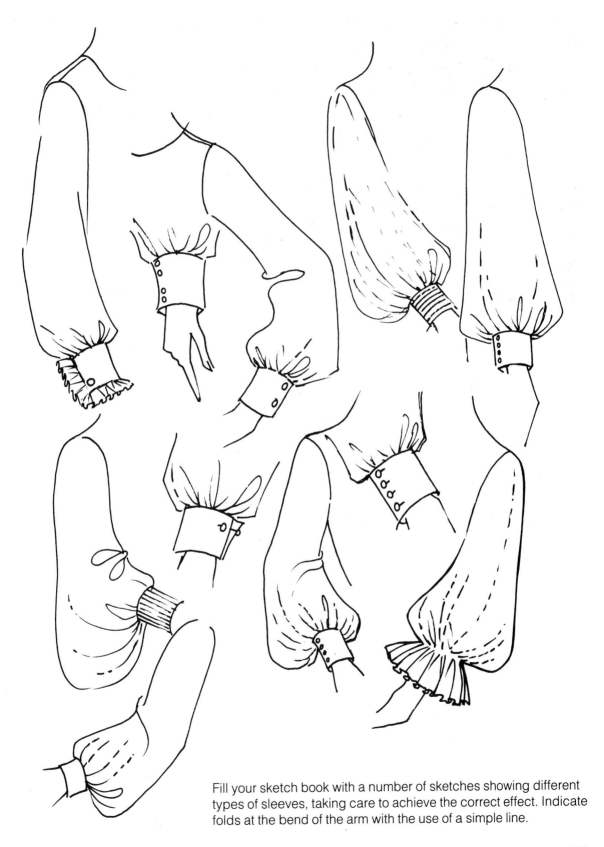

Fill your sketch book with a number of sketches showing different types of sleeves, taking care to achieve the correct effect. Indicate folds at the bend of the arm with the use of a simple line.

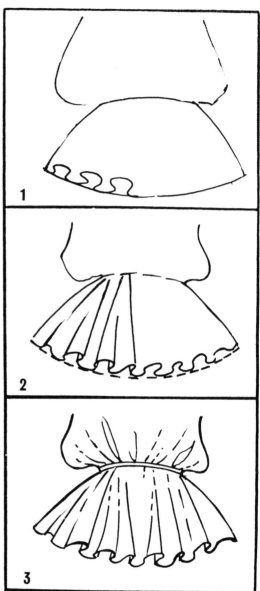

Follow the three stages as illustrated above. Notice the hemline and the effect of soft folds. Practise sketching variations of this sleeve.

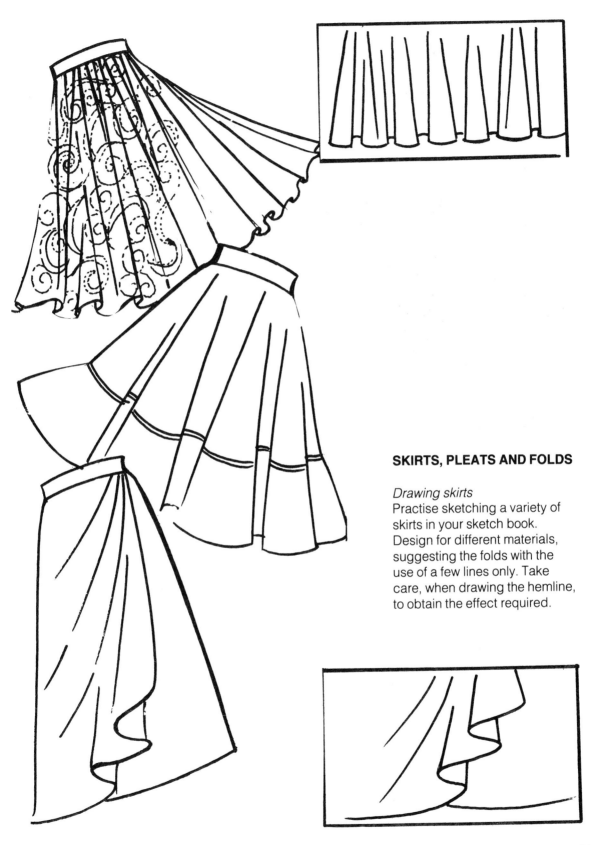

SKIRTS, PLEATS AND FOLDS

Drawing skirts
Practise sketching a variety of
skirts in your sketch book.
Design for different materials,
suggesting the folds with the
use of a few lines only. Take
care, when drawing the hemline,
to obtain the effect required.

It is good practice to keep fashion notes in your sketch book. Note the current and future trends and design some fashion images incorporating skirts of various styles.

Develop a free style of sketching, using a pen, pencil or whatever you feel most at ease with. When reporting fashions after attending a show, you will need to work quickly, so it is often a good idea to take notes and make sketches whilst watching the show.

Sketches produced with a fine fibre-tipped pen and black crayon.

Pleats
1 Inverted pleats
2 Knife pleats
3 Box pleats
4 Accordion pleats

Drapery and folds
Notice the different characteristics of the hemlines – the way the
material falls, depending on the cut and weight of the material itself.

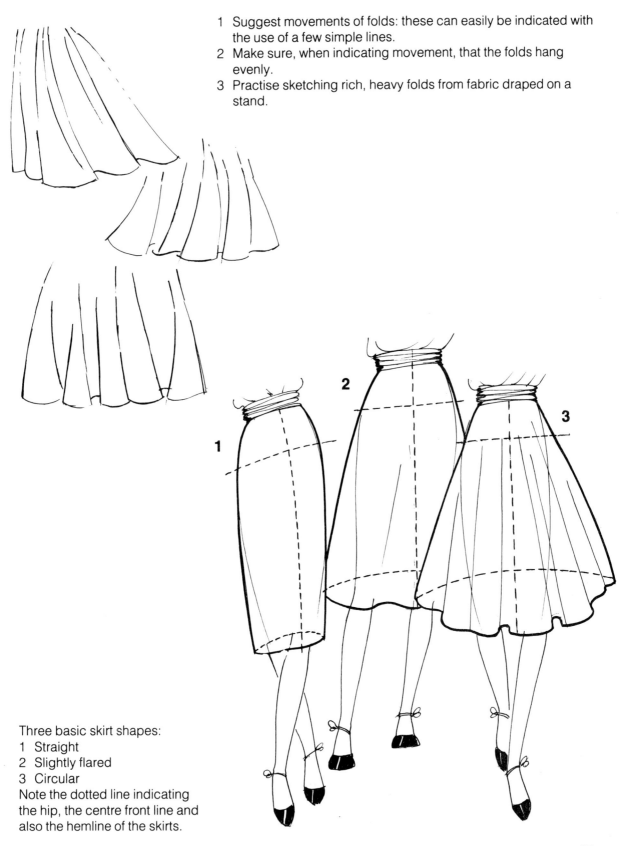

1 Suggest movements of folds: these can easily be indicated with the use of a few simple lines.
2 Make sure, when indicating movement, that the folds hang evenly.
3 Practise sketching rich, heavy folds from fabric draped on a stand.

Three basic skirt shapes:
1 Straight
2 Slightly flared
3 Circular
Note the dotted line indicating the hip, the centre front line and also the hemline of the skirts.

When sketching folds and drapery it is good practice to drape lengths of fabric on a dress stand, noting the behaviour of the fabric and the way in which it falls.

Refer to photographs illustrating dresses incoporating gathers, folds, pleats etc, and also make sketches from costume on display in museums.

Fashions seen at Ascot, 1905

Techniques in Creating Textures and Patterns

USING DIFFERENT MEDIA

Collect paints, pens, pencils, crayons etc and experiment with any new materials that are introduced. Keep the materials stored in a box so they are easy for you to use. A small tool box or a fishing box is useful for this purpose and may be purchased at a reasonable price. Make sure all tops are replaced on felt- and fibre-tipped pens as they tend to dry out when the caps are left off them. Clean all your brushes out when you have finished using them and make sure you never leave them in the water jar for a long time.

Keep a clean pallet for mixing your paints; old dishes or tiles are useful. Felt pens and tubes of watercolour paint can be kept in small plastic bags or boxes. Rotring pens need careful looking after; if you make sure they are clean after using it will save a great deal of trouble when you next wish to use them.

Experiment with your materials, combining different media to achieve effects. Use paper of differrent textures and surface weights. It is not always the most expensive materials that necessarily give the best results.

Keep a reference file of any experiments you may make with your materials. It will prove most useful when working on your design projects.

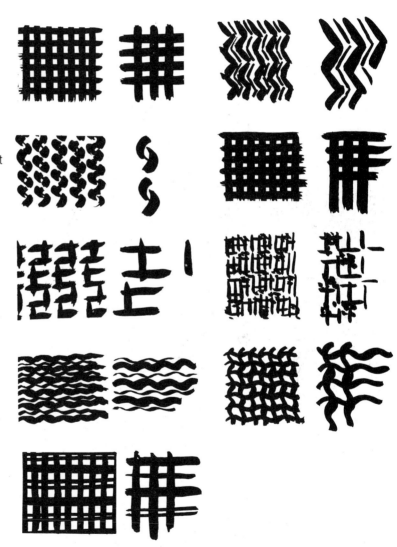

As an exercise, take a selection of fabric samples and work from them. Study the principal characteristics of the fabric, and suggest the weave and the pattern in your drawing. On this page is a selection of weaves, showing how an effect can be achieved with a few brush strokes.

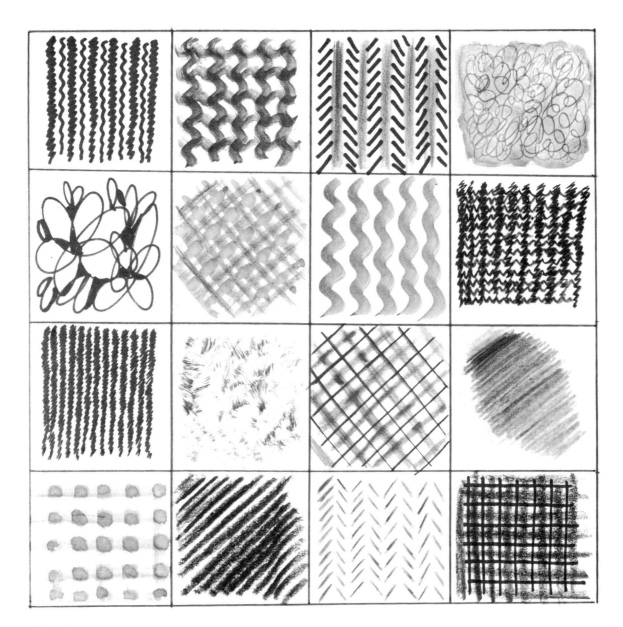

Exercise

Take a sheet of paper, square it off into sections and experiment in each square, creating different textures and patterns. Use a selection of pens, paints, crayons, and inks. Try the effects of tweeds, fur, knitted textures and patterns, working from samples you have collected; you can also create some textures and patterns of your own. This type of sheet will be most useful as a reference in your folder. Make notes on how certain effects were achieved: by using candle wax, working on wet paper, or scratching into a wet surface with the end of a paint brush.

Fashion sketch illustrating a selection of different surface effects and textures incorporated in one design. The fur top was achieved with black watercolour paint applied with a dry brush on a rough textured paper. The jumper was drawn with a thick, black pencil using different line values. The black leather belt was painted, leaving areas of white to suggest soft folds of leather. The tweed skirt was drawn in a black crayon, suggesting folds with a watercolour wash of grey. The knitted stockings were drawn in black soft pencil, the leather boots in watercolour wash.

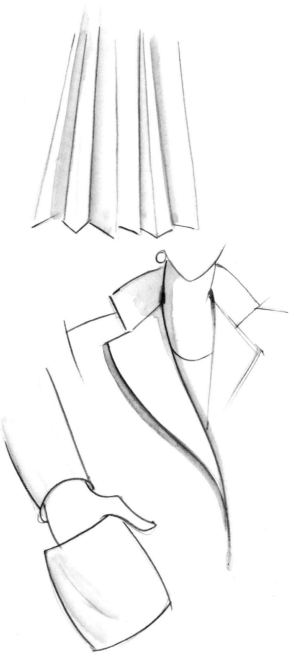

Blazer and skirt produced with a line and wash effect. The line was sketched in first with a 3B pencil, then a watercolour wash of black was applied, using a lot of water, to areas of the design to suggest shadows. When using this effect, always consider where the light is falling. The surface of the illustration paper used was very smooth.

A selection of fashion sketches experimenting with different pens and tone effects. Make a selection of sketches using pens of different thicknesses. Try stylized effects of poses and faces to suggest the mood of a fashion.

Fine Rotring pen and watercolour wash for tone

Black fibre-tipped pen

Thick black fibre-pointed pen

Ball-point pen

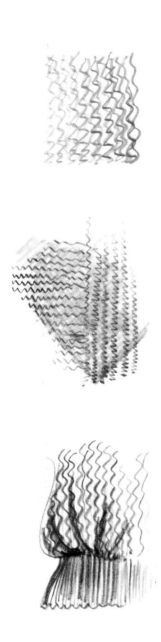

Knitted garments suggesting patterns. The effects were obtained with a soft Royal Sovereign Black Prince pencil working on a smooth surface illustration card. Different pressures and points of the pencil were used to achieve contrast in tone.

Experiment with pencil, creating different effects, before working on your designs.

Evening jacket, skirt and lace top. Note the folds and gathers in the jacket and skirt with the contrast of the lace top.

The effects were achieved with a watercolour wash run over the areas of shadow. The lace top is a combination of pencil, pen and wash.

Rotring pen and watercolour wash

Practise drawing folds, gathers and drapes using different paints, pencils, pens etc. Transparent fabrics are suggested with a fine Rotring pen and watercolour wash.

Make sketches of folds, working from fabric draped on a dress stand or on a model, if possible. Study the folds and the behaviour of different fabrics from a fine silk to a heavy tweed.

Techniques of Layout and Presentation

Presentation drawings and a general display of work are called for when a designer is showing a collection of designs to a client. For a student this will be important for examinations, assessments, competitions, and interviews.

The way in which the work is presented may vary considerably. A stylized drawing technique can be used or alternatively a more realistic approach.

The work may be mounted in several different ways; flat mounting onto card with the aid of mounting glue, or window mounting, i.e. cutting the mount out and displaying the drawing in the space created; alternatively transparent folders can be used.

The composition of the design sheet, and the arrangement of figures, notes and fabric samples, needs careful consideration. It is advisable to rough out in your sketch book a numbr of possibilities before deciding on the composition to be used. A background and decorative effects may be used with discretion, but never let the effects of decoration overpower the designs.

1

2

3

4

When considering a layout for a presentation sheet it is useful to experiment with a selection of different arrangements before making a final decision.

Work out ideas in your sketch book or on sheets of paper, considering the different possibilities of arranging your figures, fabrics and notes and giving detailed information when required.

Note the way the ideas illustrated show four variations of layout for the presentation of a suit:

1 Figures, front and back views, drawing from head to hem of skirt fitted into the box with fabrics grouped freely.

2 Full-length figures arranged to display the total look. Note the simple line, giving emphasis to the figures. The fabric and notes have been placed at the side, balancing the figures.

3 Figure placed to the side of the box and drawn from head to hemline, balanced by the clear working drawing on the left. The fabric has been placed with the working drawings.

4 Figure placed to the side of the sheet. The working drawings are in the background. The curved line gives added interest and leads the eye to the main figure.

Completed presentation drawing in line produced with a fine pointed fibre-tipped pen, showing the back and front view with sample fabrics attached. The simple shape has been added behind the figures to bring the composition together. This style of drawing, produced with a simple black line, is excellent for photocopying to send out to buyers.

1

3

jacket with shawl
collar cut very
narrow. Raglan
sleeve ¾ length
with contrasting
cuff. Jacket cut
very full drawn in
at the waist with
a wide belt.
Skirt cut with a
slight flair and
wrap over style

2

Three stages of a presentation drawing:

1 Consider the most attractive layout to present the design. It is helpful to develop a few possible layouts in your sketch book before deciding on the final arrangements. The pose of the figure should reflect the feeling and occasion in which the design would be worn, e.g. elegant, sporty, casual, sophisticated, etc.

2 Lightly sketch the figures with a pencil within the planned space, considering the arrangements of the front and back views in relation to one another.

3 In the background a shape has been placed in a sharp contrasting shade to give emphasis to the shape of the jacket. The sample fabrics and notes have been arranged on the sheet to balance the composition.

Four different arrangements of a presentation sheet using a contrasting colour in the background to offset the figures.

Exercise
Select some of your designs and experiment with different arrangements. Work within a shape, sketching freely as illustrated.

Two stages of presentation drawing, using a number of felt pens of different thickness and a grey magic marker pen for tone effects and background shape (fashions from 1978-9).

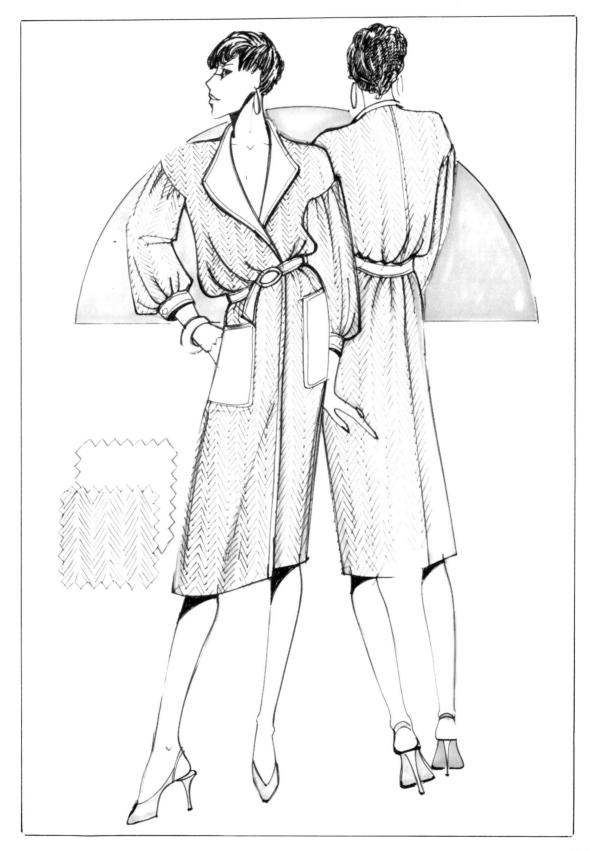

Beach outfit – note the arrangement of the two figures and the simple background which completes the composition. The drawing has been produced with a felt-tipped pen, the finer line with a Rotring pen, and the tone with a watercolour wash.

Two stages of a fashion sketch, drawn with a fibre-pointed black pen and magic marker. Note the construction lines used to balance the sketch and the way in which the herringbone tweed of the trousers has been developed.

Design presentation drawing of a jacket and trousers worn with a knitted top. The layout shows a fashion sketch of the complete outfit and a clear, diagrammatic line drawing of the outfit illustrating the back and front views together with sample fabrics.

Full-length evening skirt and lace top with evening coat. The skirt and coat are of jersey silk. The effect has been achieved with two black pencils of different thickness using a variation of pressure and a watercolour wash applied over the pencil shading for the folds and gathers. The lace is a combination of black ink and watercolour.

Experiment in your design drawings with a variety
of poses; try different hairstyles and vary your
techniques, using a combination of pens, paints
and inks. The three sketches illustrate the same
design, using a water solvent felt-tipped pen, and
water applied with a brush, causing the ink to run.

A selection of rough layouts for the presentation sheet. It is very important to make the design easy to understand and to give complete information by the use of the sketches, notes and sample fabrics.

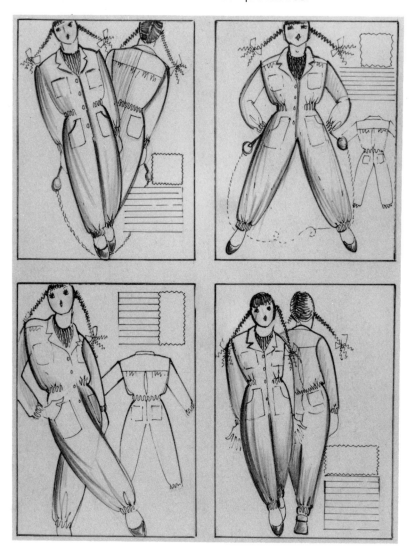

Presentation drawing of a child's jumpsuit showing front and back views. The front view has been coloured and in contrast the back has been left as a simple line. Note the figures arranged against the solid colour shape and the areas below allocated for the sample fabrics and notes.

Playsuit with front
button fastening, set in
sleeves, patch pockets
and elasticated at waist
wrist and hem of trousers

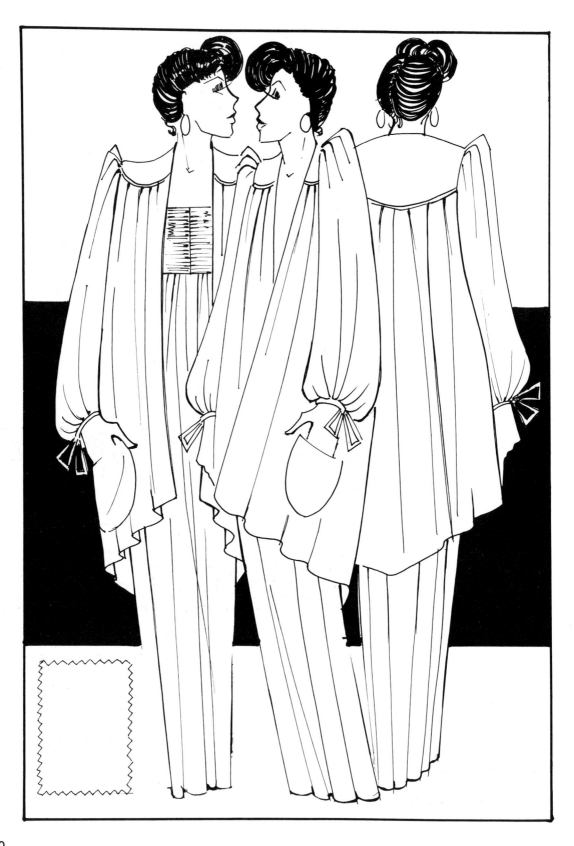

Jacket with
shoulder yoke,
set in sleeves
narrow collar
and belt. Worn
with accordion
pleated skirt.

Presentation drawing of a short evening dress and jacket, showing three views. This is a simple line drawing using fibre-tipped pen. Note the way the folds and gathers have been indicated. The drawing has been produced on a smooth surface white card.

Presentation drawing of a jacket, skirt and top, produced with watercolour wash, fibre-point pen and finer details added with a Rotring pen. Note the arrangement of the figures in the background against the simple decorative panel and the placement of the fabric and detail notes.

Presentation drawing of a suit and blouse. Note the use of the simple shape in the background and the arrangement of the figures and fabric samples to complete the compisition.

Presentation drawing flat-mounted using a panel of colour to display the figures.

Presentation drawing window-mounted. Note the arrangement of the three figures against a shape of contrasting colour.

Presentation drawing produced with a thick black crayon pencil.

DISPLAYING WORK FOR EXHIBITIONS

Before arranging a display of your work for assessment or an exhibition, consider carefully the space available on the screens to obtain the best results. It will help to plan your display through a number of sketches before deciding on the final arrangement, relating the size of the drawings, samples and garments to the size of the screens available.

The colour of the screens, and of the mounting card also has to be considered, as well as the lettering used.

Plan the way the portfolios of work are arranged as well as the samples, making the presentation easy to view.

Be careful when displaying garments not to distort the design by using too many pins. It is more practical to display garments on hangers or stands if possible. This will make it easier for the examiner to assess the work.

Fashion Illustration for Advertising

The fashion illustrator works in advertising, producing drawings for sales promotion, magazine articles, newspapers, and publicity material for stores and catalogues. Fashion drawings are often used for display purposes. Another area of work is in producing trend sketches for fashion information services, forecasting future trends, and producing sketches at fashion shows. The fashion illustrator is usually trained as a graphic designer. However, many illustrators start fashion drawing while taking a fashion design course.

When producing material for a client the fashion illustrator is given a brief from which to work. This indicates the space allocated for the drawing, in the case of an advertisement, and the layout of the page. The technique to be used is specified – line, line and tone, two colours or more – and often also the fashion image to be projected, for example a particular type of person to whom the drawing must appeal.

Styles of drawing vary considerably. The glossy magazines and stores with a high fashion image tend to use the more elegant and free-style drawings. These illustrations are usually drawn in a very individual manner, often only giving an impression of a look, but projecting a strong feeling of a fashion.

For the big department stores and fashion catalogues an accurate representation of the merchandise advertised is required.

The styles of drawing are constantly changing and reflecting the influences and mood of fashion at a particular time. They may vary from the very stylized techniques which were fashionable during the 1960s to the more realistic style which is currently popular.

It is important to keep constantly in tune with the general feeling in fashion, noting any new details which project the right image e.g. hairstyles, make-up, and general accessories.

Fashion plate of c. 1937-8. When developing and designing ideas with reference to past fashions, illustrations of this kind can be a useful source of inspiration. Note the details of the fashion plates illustrated, ie drapes, bias cut, decorative stitching etc.

17010

17010 A

Fashion plate of
c. 1937-8

17042

17042 A

Artists' Materials

You should work with new materials whenever possible, experimenting to achieve different effects. It is not always necessary to spend much money to obtain the best results. The materials listed range from the basic to the sophisticated.

PAPER AND BOARD

Cartridge paper is white and has a finely grained surface suitable for pencil, paint, crayon and charcoal. It is made in several different thicknesses and qualities.

Coloured cartridge paper has a slightly textured surface and is suitable for watercolour, pastels, and coloured pencils.

Cartridge drawing pads with stiff cardboard backs are obtainable in a range of sizes.

Cartridge sketch pads with stiff cardboard backs are obtainable in a range of sizes.

Layout pads contain white semi-transparent detail paper with a surface ideal for pencil, ink or crayon.

Watercolour paper is especially made for watercolour painting and can have either a smooth or a rough surface. Many different qualities are available in pad or book form.

Ingres paper is ideal for pastel and tempera work. You can buy a large selection of colours in sheets or as a pad.

Bound sketch books are made in different sizes and qualities of paper.

Illustration board – different sizes and thicknesses are available with a variety of surfaces which will take ink, gouache, watercolour, charcoal and crayon.

Coloured mounting board is a smooth dull-surfaced board suitable for mounting work. A large selection of colours is available in different sizes and thicknesses.

Bristol board has a smooth white surface suitable for pen and ink work.

PENCILS AND CRAYONS

Drawing pencils – a pencil's degree of hardness is printed on it in a standard code: 6B is very soft; 9H very hard; F and HB are medium; EX is extremely soft.

Charcoal pencils will give the same effect as pure charcoal sticks. They are non scratch and non glossy and available in hard, medium and soft.

Coloured pencils can be bought in boxes or separately in a wide range of colours. Some makes are water soluble which enables you to wash over the pencil stroke with a paint brush, giving the effect of painting.

Crayons – wax crayons can be most effective in fashion sketches. There is a good selection of colours and thicknesses.

ERASERS

Kneaded erasers – soft putty rubbers that can be moulded to a point, and used for pastel, charcoal and pencil.

Soft erasers are used for pencil lead or surface cleaning.

Paper cleaner or gum eraser is a pliable soft eraser gum which wears away during use but does not damage the paper surface.

DRAWING PENS

Many different drawing pens are available. Listed below are a few of them, selected for their different effects.

Rotring – technical pens have a drawing point which may be replaced with different sizes. They are designed for easy refilling.

The Pelikan Technos drawing pen is a cartridge filled drawing pen with points designed for different types of art work e.g. stencilling, ruling and free-hand work.

Osmiroid Sketch fountain pen – a less expensive pen which provides a variety of line values from bold to fine. The pen has a reservoir to maintain a constant ink flow.

Pen holders and nibs – a selection of plastic or wood pen holders and different size nibs are made for use with coloured or black indian ink and are cheaper than the other pens listed.

Marker pens – there are two basic types: spirit and water. The line thicknesses can vary from very fine to broad. The tips are either nylon, fibre or felt.

Magic Markers are made in many colours and are quick drying. The ink flows smoothly through a wedge shaped felt nib. Colours can be mixed by superimposition. Fine line markers are also available in corresponding colours.

Stabito fibre-tips come in a good range of colours with a shaped tip to give you a fine line used upright and a broad side for filling in large areas. Available in sets or individually.

COLOURS

Pastels – a large range of colours and different qualities are obtainable. The prices vary with the quality.

Designer's gouache colours, sold in tubes, are excellent for their outstanding brilliance and exceptionally smooth flow. They will produce combinations of transparency and opacity.

Drawing inks – all inks can be used equally well with brush or pen and may be diluted with distilled water. Because they contain shellac a second coat may be superimposed without disturbing the first.

Watercolours – boxes of students' or artists' watercolours are sold in a range of sizes. They are also available in tubes.

BRUSHES

The best quality brushes are still made by hand which means that they are very expensive. Many sizes and qualities are available from sable hair and ox hair to squirrel, which is cheaper. Hog hair is used to make brushes for oil painting because of its strength and ability to hold oil paint. Recently, cheaper synthetic hair brushes have become available. Always clean your brushes immediately after use. Shape up hairs after cleaning and never leave brushes resting on their bristles.

ADHESIVES

Cow Gum is a transparent rubber solution sold in tubes or tins for mounting photographs and pasting up work.

Pritt is a non greasy adhesive which is suitable for sticking fabric.

Copydex is an extra strong latex adhesive suitable for paper and fabric.

Spray Mount is sold in aerosol cans for mounting work. It gives an instant all over tack and wrinkle-free bond even on the thinnest paper. Mounted work can be unstuck.

Photo mount – a permanent adhesive for mounting photographs which is colourless, quick to apply and easy to control.

MISCELLANEOUS

Drawing boards are usually made of wood in a variety of sizes.

Portfolios – stiff durable portfolios are made from resistant simulated fabric. The corners, gusset and hinged flaps are reinforced with strong cloth.

Black leathercloth portfolios, with zip closings, are used by professional designers – the work is displayed in transparent pockets which are held in a ring binder.

Presentation books have hard plastic covers and contain clear acetate pockets. They are used for protecting and displaying work.

Protective sprays – it is often a good idea to protect your work against accidental damage with a protective spray. The spray effects are either matt or glossy.

Book List

Most of these books can be obtained through public and college libraries.

FIGURE DRAWING

CRONEY, John, *Anthropometry for Designers,* Batsford 1982

CRONEY, John, *Drawing Figure Movement,* Batsford 1983

GORDON, Louise, *Anatomy and Figure Drawing,* Batsford 1979

GORDON, Louise, *Drawing the Human Head,* Batsford 1977

LOOMIS, Andrew, *Drawing the Head and Hands,* Chapman & Hall 1956

LOOMIS, Andrew, *Figure Drawing for All its Worth,* Viking Press 1971

MUYBRIDGE, Edward, *The Human Figure in Motion,* Dover 1955

SHEPPARD, Joseph, *Anatomy: A Complete Guide for Artists*, Pitman 1975

SHEPPARD, Joseph, *Drawing the Female Figure,* Pitman 1975

FASHION DESIGN AND ILLUSTRATION

COULDRIDGE, Alan, *The Hat Book,* Batsford 1982

IRELAND, Patrick, J., *Basic Fashion Design,* Batsford 1972

IRELAND, Patrick J., *Drawing and Designing Children's and Teenage Fashions,* Batsford 1979

IRELAND, Patrick J., *Drawing and Designing Menswear,* Batsford 1976.

IRELAND, Patrick J., *Fashion Design,* Cambridge University Press 1979

IRELAND, Patrick J., *Fashion Drawing for Advertising,* Batsford 1974

NAYLOR, Brenda, *Technique of Fashion Design,* Batsford 1975

NICHOLAS, Annwen & TEAGUE, Daphne, *Embroidery in Fashion,* Pitman 1975

PHILIPSON, Norman, *Creative Design for Fashion and Embroidery,* Studio Vista 1976

ROBINSON, Julian, *The Golden Age of Style,* Orbis 1976

SLOANE, Eunice M., *Illustrating Fashion,* Harper & Row 1977

TWENTIETH-CENTURY FASHION

BATTERSBY, Martin, *Art deco fashion: French Designers 1908-1925,* Academy 1974

BERNARD, Barbara, *Fashion in the 60s,* Academy 1978

BLACK, J., & GARLAND, Madge, *A History of Fashion,* Orbis 1975

CARTER, Ernestine, *The Changing World of Fashion,* Weidenfeld & Nicholson 1977

DORNER, Jane, *Fashion: the Changing Shape of Fashion through the Years,* Octopus 1974

EWING, Elizabeth, *History of Twentieth-Century Fashion,* Batsford 1975

HOWELL, Georgina, *In Vogue,* Allen Lane 1975

PEACOCK, John, *Fashion Sketchbook 1920-1960,* Thames & Hudson 1977

ROBINSON, Julian, *Fashion in the forties,* Academy 1976

ROBINSON, Julian, *Fashion in the thirties,* Oresko 1978

SICHEL, Marion, *Costume Reference* series, Vols 7-10, Batsford 1978/9

PATTERN CUTTING

NEALMS, *Fashion and Clothing Technology,* Hulton Educational Publications

SHOBEN, Martin & WARD, Janet, *Pattern Cutting and Making Up: The Professional Approach,* Vols 1-3, Batsford 1980/81

STANLEY, Helen, *Modelling and Flat Cutting For Fashion,* Hutchinson, 1981

Areas of Research and Study

Observe the current fashion trends at fashion shows, exhibitions and selected window displays, as well as in general advertising features in glossy magazines. Keep constantly in touch with the feeling of fashion and the influences that are affecting it – trends in the social climate such as music, films, theatre, and new leisure and sport activities.

Samples – if you are able to sew and can produce samples of embroidery and fabric effects such as smocking, quilting, and appliqué it is helpful to use the samples when drawing to obtain the correct effects. They are also useful as a source of inspiration when designing.

Read as many current fashion magazines as possible, as well as books on the history of costume, decoration, and embroidery. Study text books on textiles, cutting patterns, modelling on the stand, and other suggested areas of study.

Sketch from life, when possible making sketches from a model. Drape fabrics on a dress stand, noting the behaviour of the different fabrics and the way in which each falls and gathers. Sketch freely in your sketch book, making notes of anything of interest for future reference. Make sketches when visiting museums and costume exhibitions.

Collect cuttings of fashion articles and photographs from periodicals. Select postcards from exhibitions, museums and art galleries which interest you. Keep a collection of sample fabrics knitting yarns and trimmings. Make a folder of fashion illustrations that appeal to you. Many reproductions of the work of past illustrators are available in the form of postcards and prints.

The fashion influences of a romantic, 'country' look.